MY FIRST BOOK
URUGUAY

ALL ABOUT URUGUAY FOR KIDS

Copyright 2023 by Globed Children Books

All rights reserved. No part of this book may be reproduced or distributed in any form without prior written permission from the author, with the exception of non-commercial uses permitted by copyright law.

Limited of Liability/Disclaimer of Warranty: The publisher and author make no representations or liabilities with respect to the accuracy and completeness of the contents of this work and specifically disclaim all warranties including without limitations warranties of fitness of particular purpose. No warranty may be created or extended by sales or promotional materials. This work is sold with the understanding that the publisher and author is not engaging in rendering medical, legal or any other professional advice or service. Further, readers should be aware that websites listed in this work may have changed or disappeared between when this work was written and when it is read.

Interior and cover Design: Daniel Day
Editor: Margaret Bam

For My Sons, Daniel, David and Jude

Main Square in Montevideo, Plaza la Indepencia

Uruguay

Uruguay is a **country**.

A country is land that is controlled by a **single government**. Countries are also called **nations, states, or nation-states**.

Countries can be **different sizes**. Some countries are big and others are small.

City of Punta del Este

Where Is Uruguay?

Uruguay is located in the continent of **South America**.

A continent is **a massive area of land that is separated from others by water or other natural features**.

Uruguay is situated in the southern part of South America.

Montevideo Cityscape, Uruguay

Capital

The capital of Uruguay is Montevideo.

Montevideo is located in the **southern part** of the country.

Montevideo is the largest city in Uruguay.

Piriapolis, Uruguay

Departments

Uruguay is a country that is made up of 19 departments

The regions of Uruguay are as follows:

Artigas, Canelones, Cerro Largo, Colonia, Durazno, Flores, Florida, Lavalleja, Maldonado, Montevideo, Paysandú, Río Negro, Rivera, Rocha, Salto, San José, Soriano, Tacuarembó and Treinta y Tres.

Montevideo, Uruguay

Population

Uruguay has population of around **3 million people** making it the 132th most populated country in the world and the 10th most populated country in South America.

About 95% of the population lives in urban areas, with the majority residing in the southern coastal region.

Candombe Mural, Ciudad Vieja District, Montevideo

Size

Uruguay is **181,034 square kilometres** making it the 11th largest country in South America by area and the 89th largest country in the world.

Uruguay borders two countries: Brazil to the north and Argentina to the west.

Cerrito, Montevideo, Uruguay

Languages

The official language of Uruguay is Spanish. The Spanish language is spoken by hundreds of millions of people across the world.

Uruguayan Sign Language is the deaf sign language of Uruguay and has been used since 1910.

Here are a few Spanish phrases
- **¿Cómo estás?** - How are you?
- **Mucho gusto** - Nice to meet you
- **De nada** - You're welcome

Salto del Penitente, Uruguay

Attractions

There are lots of interesting places to see in Uruguay.

Some beautiful places to visit in Uruguay are

- **Solis Theater**
- **Puerto Market**
- **Salvo Palace**
- **Montevideo Metropolitan Cathedral**
- **Fortress of Santa Teresa**
- **Salto del Penitente**

Punta del Este, Uruguay

History of Uruguay

Uruguay has a rich history that spans back over 10,000 years. The country's original inhabitants were indigenous tribes, including the Charrua, Guaraní, and Chaná people.

In the 16th century, Spanish conquistadors arrived in the region and established colonies. Uruguay became independent of Spain in 1811 and was annexed by Brazil until 1825.

Following a three-year federation with Argentina, Uruguay became an independent nation in 1828.

Customs in Uruguay

Uruguay has many fascinating customs and traditions.

- **Yerba Mate is a traditional drink and forms a central part of Uruguayan culture. It is often shared among friends and family, and is considered a symbol of hospitality.**
- **The carnival in Uruguay is one of the largest and most colourful in South America. It takes place in February or March and features music, dancing, and elaborate costumes.**
- **Candombe is a traditional Afro-Uruguayan music and dance style that is often performed during carnival and other festive occasions.**

Music of Uruguay

Uruguay has a rich musical tradition, including styles like **candombe, tango, and murga.** Candombe is a type of music and dance that originated among Afro-Uruguayan communities, while tango and murga have their roots in Argentina and Spain.

Some notable Uruguayan musicians include
- **Ruben Rada**
- **Jorge Drexler**
- **Ana Prada**
- **Martín Buscaglia**
- **Jaime Roos**

Chivito

Food of Uruguay

Uruguay is known for having delicious, flavoursome and rich dishes.

The national dish of Uruguay is **Chivito** which is a sandwich of sliced beefsteak with mozzarella, ham, tomatoes, mayonnaise and olives.

Food of Uruguay

Uruguayan cuisine is heavily influenced by European culinary traditions, particularly Spanish and Italian.

Some popular dishes in Uruguay include

- **Milanesa: A breaded and fried meat cutlet**
- **Empanadas: Pastry pockets filled with a variety of savoury ingredients**
- **Dulce de Leche: A caramel-like spread made from sweetened condensed milk**
- **Asado - A barbecue-style dish made with different cuts of meat**

Colonia del Sacramento, Uruguay

Weather in Uruguay

Uruguay has a **temperate climate**, with mild winters and hot summers. The country receives a moderate amount of rainfall throughout the year, with the wettest months being from April to November.

January is the hottest month in Uruguay.

Cattle in pasture in Uruguay

Animals of Uruguay

There are many wonderful animals in Uruguay.

Here are some animals that live in Uruguay

- **Foxes**
- **Armadillos**
- **Rodents**
- **Snakes**
- **Spiders**
- **Burrowing Owls**

Punta del Este, Uruguay

Beaches

There are many beautiful beaches in Uruguay which is one of the reasons why so many people visit this beautiful country every year. The beaches of Uruguay are among the most pristine and unspoiled in the world.

Here are some of Uruguay's beaches

- **Playa Brava**
- **Punta del Este**
- **Playa de los Pocitos, Montevideo**
- **Playa Las Grutas**
- **Playa José Ignacio**

Uruguay footbal player

Sports of Uruguay

Soccer is the most popular sport in Uruguay, and the national team is one of the most successful in the world. The sport is deeply ingrained in the culture and has a strong following among all ages.

Here are some of famous sportspeople from Uruguay

- **Luis Suárez - Football**
- **Edinson Cavani - Football**
- **Diego Lugano - Football**
- **Álvaro Pereira - Football**
- **Fernando Muslera - Football**

José Alberto "Pepe" Mujica

Famous

Uruguay has been home to many notable figures in various fields.

Here are a few examples

- **Jose Mujica: Former president of Uruguay**
- **Mario Benedetti: One of Uruguay's most famous writers**
- **Eduardo Galeano: A well-known Uruguayan writer, best known for his book "Open Veins of Latin America,"**
- **Jorge Drexler – Well known Uruguayan musician**

Montevideo, Uruguay

Something Extra...

As a little something extra, we are going to share some lesser known facts about Uruguay.

- **In 2013, Uruguay became the first country in the world to provide a laptop for every primary school student.**
- **Uruguay is a major producer and exporter of high-quality beef and is known for its traditional asado (barbecue) culture.**
- **Uruguay has the longest national anthem in the world.**

Words From the Author

We hope that you enjoyed learning about the wonderful country of Uruguay.

Uruguay is a country rich in culture and beauty, with lots of wonderful places to visit and people to meet.

We hope you continue to learn more about this wonderful nation. If you enjoyed this book, consider leaving a review!

With Love